CAMBRIDGE

A1 Movers

AUTHENTIC EXAMINATION PAPERS

3

T0349670

STUDENT'S BOOK

Cambridge University Press

www.cambridge.org/elt

Cambridge Assessment English

www.cambridgeenglish.org

Information on this title: www.cambridge.org/9781108465137

© Cambridge University Press and UCLES 2019

First published 2019

20 19 18 17 16 15 14 13 12 11 10 9

Printed in Great Britain by Ashford Colour Press Ltd.

A catalogue record for this publication is available from the British Library

ISBN 978-1-108-46513-7 Student's Book
ISBN 978-1-108-46518-2 Answer Booklet
ISBN 978-1-108-46523-6 Audio CD

Cover illustration: Leo Trinidad/Astound

Contents

Part 1
– 5 questions –

Listen and draw lines. There is one example.

Charlie   Daisy   Fred   Jane

Sally   Jack   Vicky

Part 2

– 5 questions –

Listen and write. There is one example.

Zoe's party

	Day of birthday party:	...............Saturday................
1	Number of children at the party:	....
2	Kind of birthday cake:	.................................cake
3	Kind of drinks:	some ....
4	Food at the party:	..................with vegetables
5	After the party we:	went to funfair in ....

Part 3
– 5 questions –

Which animal does each person in Anna's family like?

Listen and write a letter in each box. There is one example.

mum | B

grandpa | ☐

aunt | ☐

uncle | ☐

dad | ☐

sister | ☐

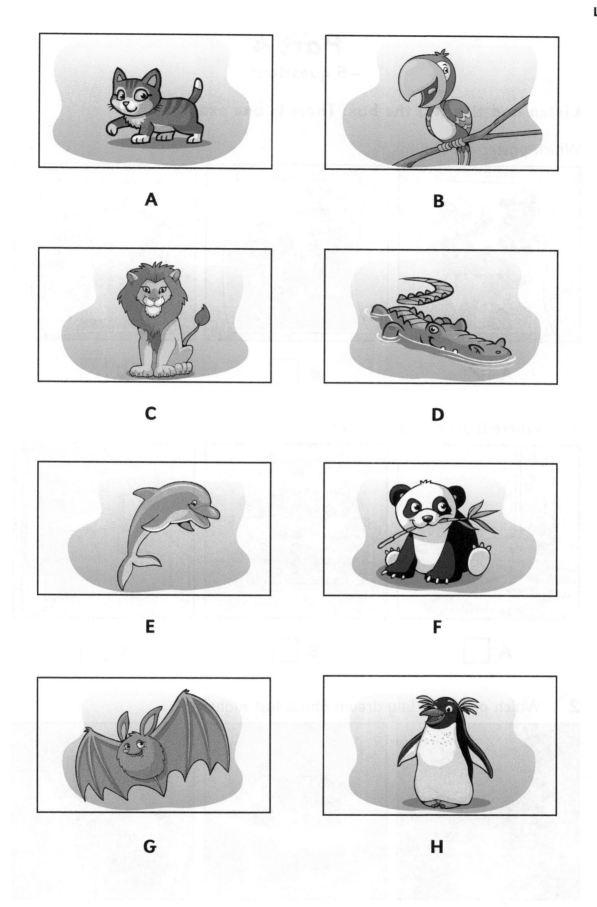

A

B

C

D

E

F

G

H

Part 4
– 5 questions –

Listen and tick (✔) the box. There is one example.

Which poster did Jim buy?

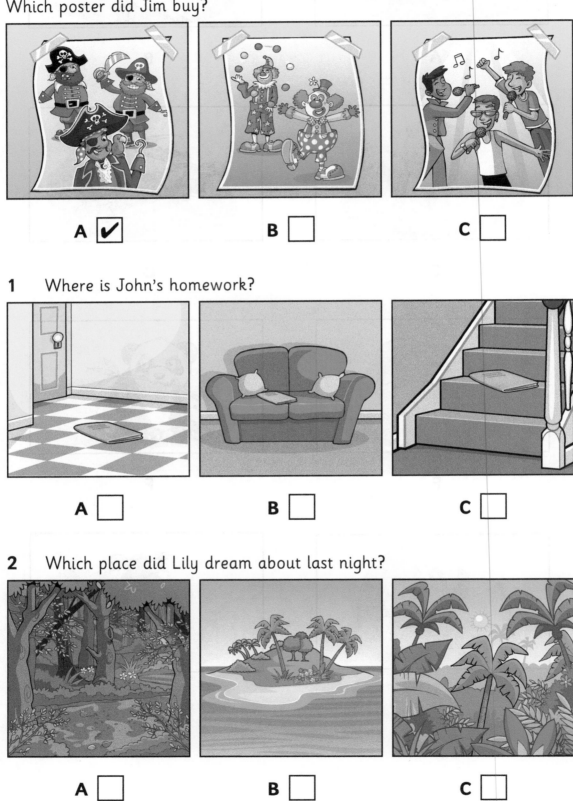

A ✔   B ☐   C ☐

1   Where is John's homework?

A ☐   B ☐   C ☐

2   Which place did Lily dream about last night?

A ☐   B ☐   C ☐

3   What is Mary doing now?

A ☐   **B** ☐   **C** ☐

4   Where did Paul lose his watch?

A ☐   **B** ☐   **C** ☐

5   Which sport did Tom do yesterday?

A ☐   **B** ☐   **C** ☐

Part 5

– 5 questions –

Listen and colour and write. There is one example.

Blank Page

Reading and Writing

Part 1

– 5 questions –

Look and read. Choose the correct words and write them on the lines. There is one example.

a shower

a funfair

a lift

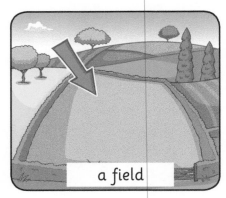

a field

the moon

a lion

a snail

a balcony

Example

You can sit outside on this part of a flat.	.... *a balcony* ....

Questions

1 This small animal can hide inside its shell.

....

2 This can take you up to another floor in a tall building.

....

3 You often see this and lots of stars in the sky at night.

....

4 Animals like sheep live here on a farm.

....

5 You can stand and wash your hair and body in this.

....

Part 2

– 6 questions –

Read the text and choose the best answer.

Example

Jim: I think this forest is a great place for a picnic.

Paul:
A Well done!
(B) So do I!
C Here you are!

Questions

1 Jim: I'm hungry now. Are you?

Paul:
A Yes, please.
B I know it is.
C Yes, I am.

2 **Jim:** Let's stop and have our picnic between these two trees

Paul:
A That's a lot!
B Good idea!
C See you!

3 **Jim:** What kind of food did you bring, Paul?

Paul:
A Salad and cold meat.
B Make a huge apple pie!
C Thanks for the sandwich.

4 **Jim:** Did you bring something to drink, too?

Paul:
A I like water more.
B We could do that.
C Only some fruit juice.

5 **Jim:** Where are the plates and cups?

Paul:
A They're inside the smaller bag.
B When Mum gave them to me.
C Yes, but they aren't here.

6 **Jim:** What shall we do after our picnic?

Paul:
A There's one by the lake.
B Let's climb a tree.
C A comic or my phone.

Part 3

– 6 questions –

Read the story. Choose a word from the box. Write the correct word next to numbers 1–5. There is one example.

My grandmother hurt her foot last Friday. She wanted a doctor to look at it. I went with her to the .... hospital ....

The doctor took off Grandma's shoe and looked at her foot very carefully.

'How did you hurt it?' he asked. 'Did you fall **(1)** .... ?'

'No,' said Grandma.

'Did you have to run to **(2)** .... a bus?' he asked.

'No, she didn't do that,' I said.

'Well, did you get out of bed too **(3)** .... ?' the doctor asked.

'No,' said my grandmother. 'I hurt it when I scored a goal.'

'It went into the back of the **(4)** .... ! She's a great football player,' I told him.

The doctor laughed. 'Well, don't worry. It's all right,' he said. 'But you must only watch football this weekend! You mustn't play it!'

'Can I go swimming in the sea?' Grandma asked. 'I love jumping in the **(5)** ....'

'No!' the doctor answered.

Example

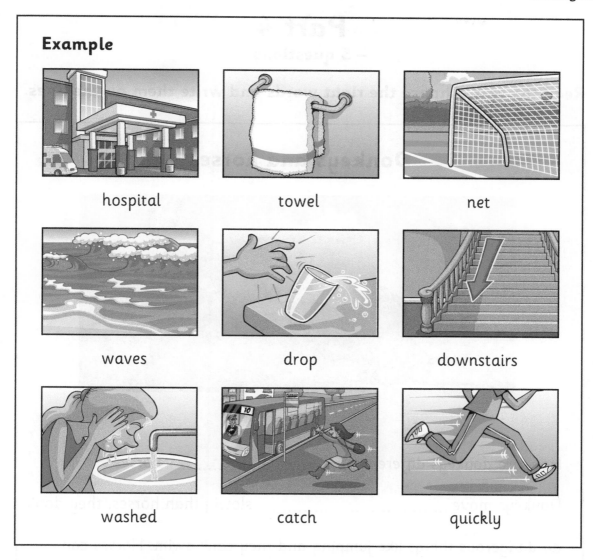

hospital

towel

net

waves

drop

downstairs

washed

catch

quickly

(6) Now choose the best name for the story.

Tick one box.

Grandma's two favourite sports!   ☐

I want to be a doctor, too!   ☐

A new pair of football boots!   ☐

Part 4
– 5 questions –

Read the text. Choose the right words and write them on the lines.

Donkeys and horses

Example How are donkeys different ....from.............. horses?

1 Donkeys move .... slowly than horses, they don't

do dangerous things like jumping and they can't swim. Horses can.

2 .... a donkey is frightened, it doesn't move. But

a horse runs!

Donkeys and horses have different ears and tails, too. A donkey has

3 .... ears than a horse, and a tail which is like

a cow's.

Most horses enjoy eating grass and live in places where it grows. Donkeys

4 can live in hot, dry places where there is .... grass.

5 But .... colours aren't very different. Most horses

and donkeys are white, black, brown or grey.

Example	from	for	with
1	more	worse	many
2	Why	When	What
3	long	longer	longest
4	no	not	nothing
5	their	them	theirs

Part 5

– 7 questions –

Look at the pictures and read the story. Write some words to complete the sentences about the story. You can use 1, 2 or 3 words.

Where's our car?

Dad and Zoe live in the city. Last Saturday, they drove into the big car park under the shopping centre. Then they walked to the sports shop. Zoe needed a new swimsuit and she found one that was really pretty. Dad bought a new tennis racket there, too.

Then they had lunch in a nice café.

Examples

Zoe and her father's home is in the .... city ....

Zoe and Dad went to the .... shopping centre .... by car.

Questions

1   Zoe found a pretty .... in the sports shop.

2   They went to a .... for their lunch.

They had pasta with tomato sauce. Then they bought lots of vegetables from the supermarket, and got some new books from the library. They walked around the pet shop, too. When Zoe smiled at a blue parrot, it said 'Hello!' to her.

At the end of the day, they had lots of bags to carry back to the car park.

3 Zoe had some .... with her pasta.

4 After they went to the supermarket and the ...., Zoe and Dad went into a pet shop.

5 Zoe and Dad had to carry .... back to the car park.

'Where's our car?' Zoe asked.

'I don't know!' said Dad. 'There are hundreds and hundreds of cars here now!'

Zoe and Dad walked up and down the car park but they couldn't find it.

'Look! There's the blue parrot again! It's on the top of one of the cars!' Zoe said.

'That's OUR car. Hooray!' Dad answered. 'What a clever parrot!'

'Happy to help!' said the parrot and then it flew off.

'Did the parrot really say that?' Mum asked when they got home.

'Yes!' Zoe laughed.

6   Zoe and Dad .... their car because there were lots of cars in the car park.

7   The .... was on the roof of Dad's car and said 'Happy to help!' when they found it!

Blank Page

Part 6
– 6 questions –

Look and read and write.

Examples

These three pirates are on an ....**island**........................ .

What is the blond pirate holding? ....**an old map**........................

Questions

Complete the sentences.

1   Someone is sleeping between the ....

2   The sun is behind the ....

Answer the questions.

3   What colour are the sails?

    ....

4   What is the whale looking at?

    ....

Now write two sentences about the picture.

5   ....

6   ....

Part 1
– 5 questions –

Listen and draw lines. There is one example.

Daisy Paul Sally Fred

Jim Vicky Charlie

Part 2
– 5 questions –

Listen and write. There is one example.

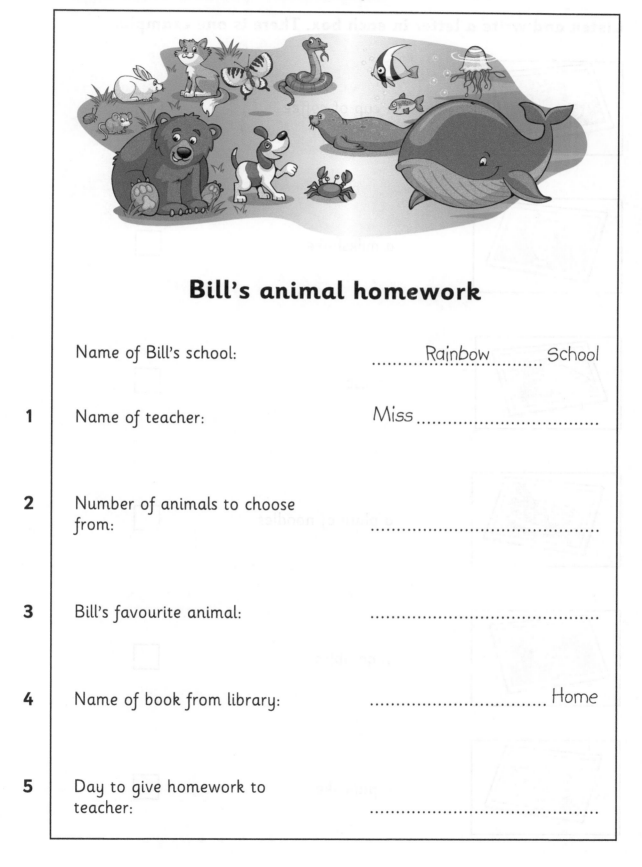

Bill's animal homework

	Name of Bill's school:	.... Rainbow .... School
1	Name of teacher:	Miss ....
2	Number of animals to choose from:	....
3	Bill's favourite animal:	....
4	Name of book from library:	.... Home
5	Day to give homework to teacher:	....

Part 3

– 5 questions –

Where did Mary find each of these pictures?

Listen and write a letter in each box. There is one example.

a cup of coffee   [F]

a milkshake   [ ]

cheese   [ ]

a plate of noodles   [ ]

vegetables   [ ]

a pancake   [ ]

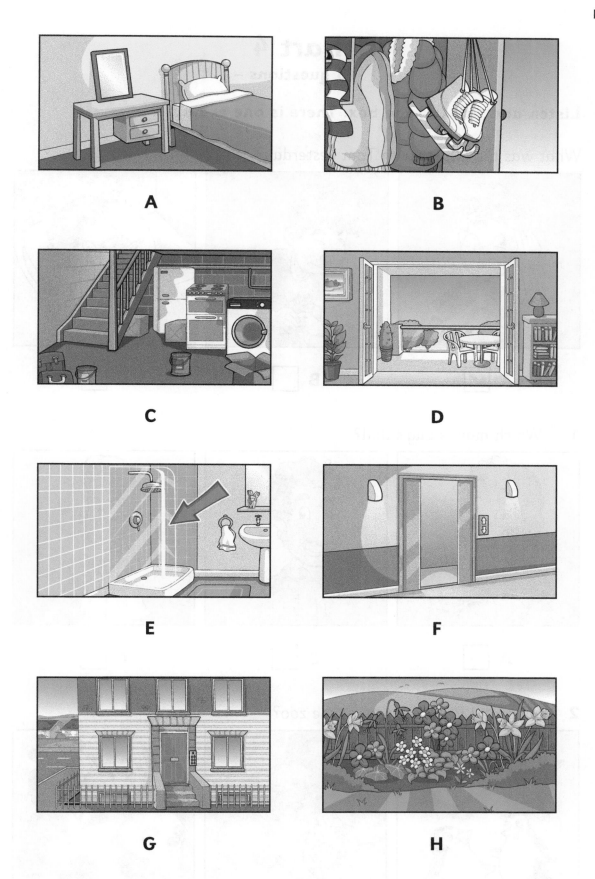

A

B

C

D

E

F

G

H

Part 4

– 5 questions –

Listen and tick (✔) the box. There is one example.

What was the matter with Tom yesterday?

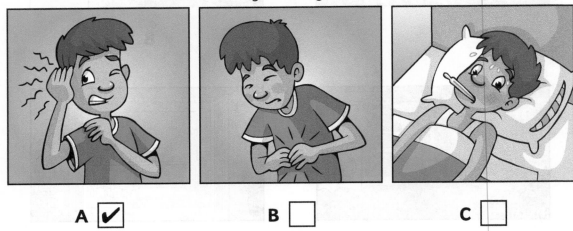

A ✔   B ☐   C ☐

1 Which man is Lily's dad?

A ☐   B ☐   C ☐

2 What did Peter see first at the zoo?

A ☐   B ☐   C ☐

3   Where is Lucy's comic?

A ☐   B ☐   C ☐

4   What is in the picnic box?

A ☐   B ☐   C ☐

5   Why are the girls laughing?

A ☐   B ☐   C ☐

Part 5

– 5 questions –

Listen and colour and write. There is one example.

Blank Page

Reading and Writing
Part 1
– 5 questions –

Look and read. Choose the correct words and write them on the lines. There is one example.

noodles

a milkshake

a sports centre

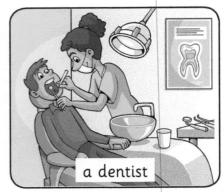
a dentist

pancakes

a funfair

a shopping centre

a film star

Example

These are long and thin and you eat
them in a bowl.

..............*noodles*..............

Questions

1 When you see this person, he or she
looks at your teeth.

....

2 You can go on scary rides with your
friends here.

....

3 You can play games like tennis or
basketball in this place.

....

4 This famous person acts in movies.

....

5 This cold drink sometimes has fruit in it.

....

Part 2

– 6 questions –

Read the text and choose the best answer.

Example

Julia:	Was it your birthday yesterday, Daisy?
Daisy:	A Yes, it was.
	B Happy Birthday!
	C Did you?

Questions

1 Julia:	What did you do on your birthday?
Daisy:	A That's a great idea.
	B It was at three o'clock.
	C We went to the circus.

2 **Julia:** What birthday presents did you get?

  Daisy:
  A   I bought a toy.
  B   Lots of different things.
  C   They're very kind.

3 **Daisy:** My grandparents gave me some ice skates.

  Julia:
  A   So do I!
  B   That's fantastic!
  C   Here you are!

4 **Julia:** Where did you go to eat yesterday?

  Daisy:
  A   We ate at a café.
  B   It's for our lunch.
  C   They're the nicest ones.

5 **Julia:** Did you have a birthday cake?

  Daisy:
  A   Eggs, milk and chocolate.
  B   Thank you! It looks very nice.
  C   Yes. My mum made it.

6 **Julia:** Was it a good birthday?

  Daisy:
  A   Yes, I did!
  B   Yes, I'm good at it!
  C   Yes, I loved it!

Part 3

– 6 questions –

Read the story. Choose a word from the box. Write the correct word next to numbers 1–5. There is one example.

Fred and Jack were on holiday with their mum and dad at the

.... *beach* .... Their dad gave them a huge ball to play with.

First, they practised **(1)** .... the ball in the water.

Then Fred said, 'This is **(2)** .... ! Let's try and play

football with it.'

It was difficult to play with a huge ball but Fred **(3)** ....

three goals.

'I love football!' he said.

'Look! The monkeys like football, too!' said Jack. He pointed to two

monkeys in a tree. 'They're watching us.'

Then Fred kicked the ball again. It flew into the **(4)** ....

behind Jack.

'I'm sorry!' said Fred.

'Don't worry,' said Jack. 'Let's go and find it.'

'There it is!' shouted Fred. 'The monkeys have got it!'

Jack laughed. 'They're playing football, too! They're very good football

players. They can **(5)** .... us to be better players!'

Example

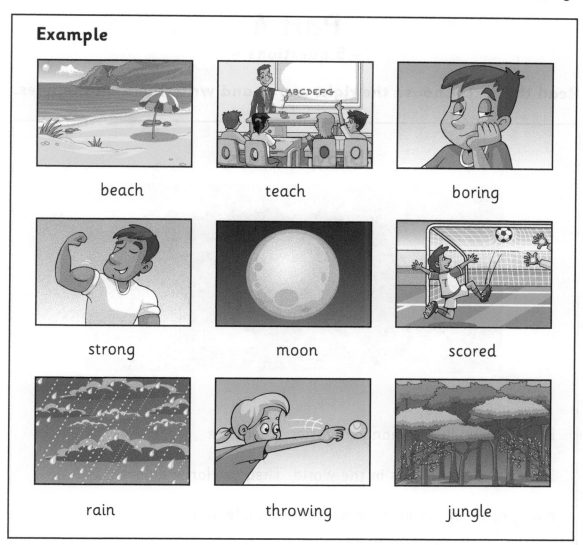

beach   teach   boring

strong   moon   scored

rain   throwing   jungle

(6)   Now choose the best name for the story.

Tick one box.

A funny football game   ☐

Fred helps the monkeys   ☐

A picnic on the beach   ☐

Part 4

– 5 questions –

Read the text. Choose the right words and write them on the lines.

Brown bears

Example

Brown bears live in many countries. There are ....about......... 200,000 brown bears in the world. They are large animals and many of them live in the mountains. People don't

1 .... see brown bears. That's because they

2 don't live in places .... there are a lot of people.

3 Brown bears are very strong. They .... rocks and small trees and then they make their homes under the ground.

4 They sleep there when it .... very cold. Brown bears eat fruit and plants. Some brown bears live near the sea.

5 .... bears eat fish and grow very big.

Example   about   after   at

1   sometimes   often   never

2   which   where   what

3   move   moved   moving

4   does   is   has

5   These   Another   This

Part 5
– 7 questions –

Look at the pictures and read the story. Write some words to complete the sentences about the story. You can use 1, 2 or 3 words.

Going to the zoo

My name is Clare and last week our class went to the zoo with our teacher, Mrs White. We had to go to school at seven-thirty in the morning to catch the bus to the zoo. It was a long drive to the zoo.

On the bus, some people sang songs and Mrs White ate her breakfast! When the bus stopped at the zoo, everyone was asleep. 'Wake up, everyone!' Mrs White called. 'Let's see the animals!'

Examples

Clare went .... to the zoo .... with her class.

Mrs White is the name of Clare's .... teacher ....

Questions

1   Mrs White had .... on the bus.

2   Clare's classmates were .... when the bus stopped at the zoo.

First, we went to see the penguins. They were brilliant! I loved watching them when they swam and played in the water. My friend, Mary, wanted to give them her sandwiches. 'Don't do that!' said Mrs White. 'You mustn't feed the animals.'

3   Clare enjoyed seeing .... when they were in
the water.

4   Mrs White didn't want the children to .... the
animals.

After that we saw the lions. They were my favourite. A man who worked at the zoo told me about them. He pointed at one of the lions. 'That's our newest lion. His name's Hugo. He came from another zoo in a big city. He likes it here because he's got lots of young lions to play with.' I took lots of photos of Hugo and I put them on the school website. Everyone loved them!

5   Clare liked the .... best.

6   Hugo was happy at the zoo because he could ....
the other lions.

7   Clare put the photos that she took of Hugo on ....

Blank Page

Part 6
– 6 questions –

Look and read and write.

Examples

The woman is carrying some ....vegetables............ .

What is the farmer driving? ....a red tractor............

Questions

Complete the sentences.

1   The birds are flying next to ....

2   Two cows are ....

Answer the questions.

3   What is the girl wearing?

     ....

4   What is the dog sitting on?

     ....

Now write two sentences about the picture.

5   ....

6   ....

Part 1
– 5 questions –

Listen and draw lines. There is one example.

Fred   Clare   Jane   Charlie

Jim   Daisy   Zoe

Part 2

– 5 questions –

Listen and write. There is one example.

Going to the farm

Name of the farm: Forest .... Farm ....

1   The children want to ride on the: ....

2   Children can give food to the: ....

3   Name of the new puppy: ....

4   Can eat picnic in a: ....

5   Go for a walk around the: ....

Part 3

– 5 questions –

Where does Peter's mum want Peter to put each of these things?

Listen and write a letter in each box. There is one example.

	cheese	B
	soup	
	pasta	
	sauce	
	coffee	
	vegetables	

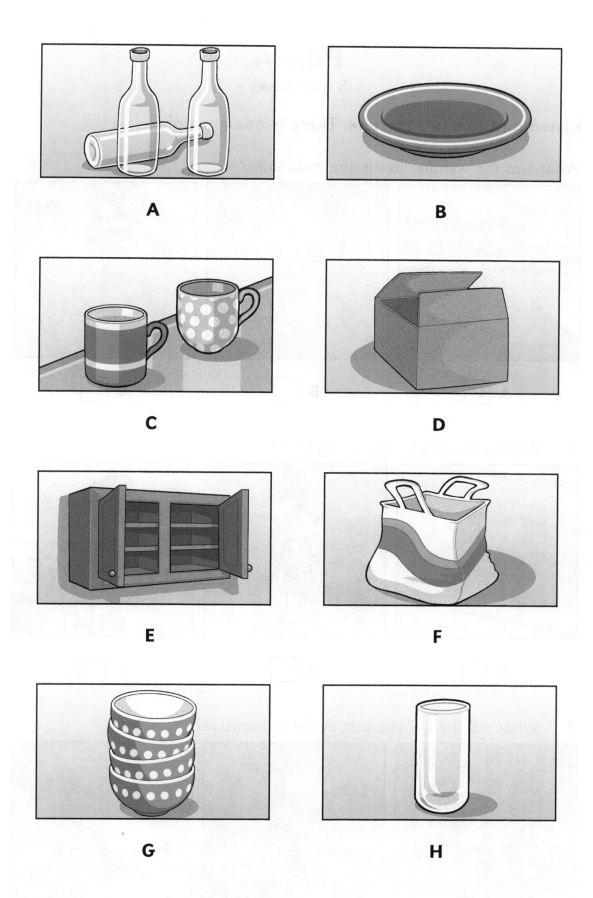

A

B

C

D

E

F

G

H

Part 4
– 5 questions –

Listen and tick (✔) the box. There is one example.

What was the weather like in the mountains?

A ✔   B ☐   C ☐

1 What is the boy's sister doing now?

A ☐   B ☐   C ☐

2 What did the girl like best in the countryside?

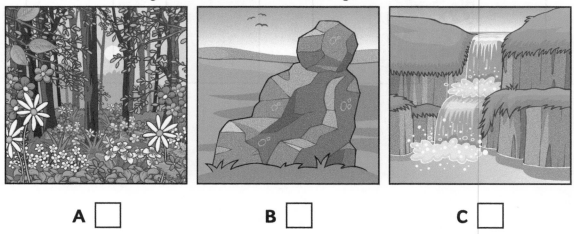

A ☐   B ☐   C ☐

3   What must the boy put in his bag now?

  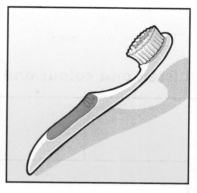

A ☐   B ☐   C ☐

4   Where does the boy live?

A ☐   B ☐   C ☐

5   What is May good at?

A ☐   B ☐   C ☐

Part 5

– 5 questions –

Listen and colour and write. There is one example.

Blank Page

Reading and Writing

Part 1
– 5 questions –

Look and read. Choose the correct words and write them on the lines. There is one example.

a funfair

coffee

a salad

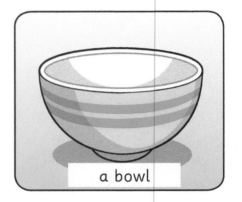

a bowl

a supermarket

a farm

a cinema

cheese

Example

This is a hot brown drink which many
grown-ups drink.

.... coffee ....

Questions

1   You can eat food like soup or ice cream
    from this.

    ....

2   People go to this place to watch films.

    ....

3   People can eat this yellow or white food
    in sandwiches or with pasta.

    ....

4   Animals like cows or sheep often live here.

    ....

5   You can buy things like food and clothes
    in this big shop.

    ....

Part 2
– 6 questions –

Read the text and choose the best answer.

Example

Jack: Was it your brother's birthday yesterday?

Julia: A   Yes, he was.
                         B   That's right.
                         C   Happy Birthday!

Questions

1   Jack: How old is your brother?

     Julia: A   Brothers are young.
                         B   He's 14 now.
                         C   No, he's older than me.

2 Jack: Did your brother have a birthday party?

Julia: A   He didn't want one this year.
                        B   What a good idea!
                        C   He's your friend too.

3 Jack: What present did you give your brother?

Julia: A   He gave it to me.
                        B   Here you are.
                        C   A book that he really wanted.

4 Jack: When is your birthday, Julia?

Julia: A   Do you like balloons?
                        B   It's this week.
                        C   There are three of them.

5 Jack: What did you do on your last birthday?

Julia: A   Birthdays are fun.
                        B   I always do that on my birthday.
                        C   I went to the circus with my family.

6 Jack: What present would you like for your birthday?

Julia: A   I don't know.
                        B   Mine is better than yours.
                        C   So do I.

Part 3
– 6 questions –

Read the story. Choose a word from the box. Write the correct word next to numbers 1–5. There is one example.

Daisy and Charlie live in a house in the ....<u>countryside</u>.......... near a

forest. The children love to play in the forest and they go there a lot. They

like to **(1)** .... trees and to hide there from their

mum and dad. One afternoon, the children were in the forest.

Then Daisy said, 'What's that noise?'

'Can you help me?' someone said.

Daisy and Charlie saw a woman. She was on the

(2) ....

'What's the matter?' asked Daisy.

'I **(3)** .... and I can't walk because my leg hurts,' the

woman said.

Daisy sat with the woman and Charlie ran to get Dad.

'Don't worry,' said Daisy. 'Our dad is very **(4)** ....

He can help you.'

Then Dad came and he **(5)** .... the woman back to

the house.

'Thank you, children,' she said. 'My name is Clare. I write books for

children. I'd like to put you in my book about the forest. Is that OK?'

'It's fantastic!' said Daisy and Charlie.

Example

countryside

hop

fell

sunny

strong

carried

climb

watered

ground

(6) **Now choose the best name for the story.**

Tick one box.

Charlie loses his sister ☐

An exciting day in the forest ☐

Daisy and Charlie help Dad ☐

Part 4
– 5 questions –

Read the text. Choose the right words and write them on the lines.

Zoos

Example Zoos can help us to learn more .... *about* .... our world.

People go to zoos to see the animals, birds and fish

1 .... come from different parts of the world.

Zoos weren't always very good places for animals

2 .... they sometimes had to live in small cages.

3 Now .... cities in the world have a big zoo.

They sometimes have long grass where animals

4 .... giraffes, lions and tigers can run and play.

5 In .... zoos, there are often rivers for the

crocodiles to swim in. The animals think they are in the

jungle – not a zoo!

Example		to	about	down
1		when	which	what
2		than	because	but
3		any	both	most
4		with	of	like
5		these	every	that

Part 5

– 7 questions –

Look at the pictures and read the story. Write some words to complete the sentences about the story. You can use 1, 2 or 3 words.

Zoe and Lucy

Zoe and Paul and their parents go to another town to see their grandparents in the holidays. They often go by car. But last week they went by train. It was a really long trip, but it wasn't boring because Paul liked looking out of the window and Zoe enjoyed drawing pictures of people on the train. She played with her doll, Lucy, too.

Examples

Zoe and Paul's grandparents live in .... *another town* ....

They often travel by .... *car* .... to their grandparents' house.

Questions

1 Last week, they went to see their grandparents by

....

2 The trip was very long, but the children didn't think it was

....

They got off the train at the station in Grandma and Grandpa's town, and they waved goodbye to the people on the train. Then Zoe said, 'Oh no! Where's Lucy?' Grandma and Grandpa helped to look for Zoe's doll but they couldn't find her. Zoe started to cry.

A man who worked at the station phoned the train driver. 'It's OK,' he said. 'The driver has got Lucy! Come here this evening to get your doll.'

Grandma said, 'Let's go to the café. We can wait for the train driver there.'

3   Zoe wasn't happy because they couldn't find her

....

4   Someone at the station .... the train driver.

5   It was Grandma's idea to .... the train driver at the café.

⇨

The family went to the café and they waited all afternoon. 'This isn't fun,' said Paul. Then Mum said, 'Look! There's the train!' 'Hooray!' they all shouted. The driver stopped the train and gave Zoe her doll. 'Now we can all go home!' said Grandma.

6 It wasn't fun at the café because the family had to wait
....

7 When the driver .... , he gave Lucy to Zoe.

Blank Page

Part 6
– 6 questions –

Look and read and write.

Examples

There are some clouds in the ....sky................... .

Where are the people? ....at the beach..............

Questions

Complete the sentences.

1   The two boys who are playing football are wearing

....

2   The cat on the blanket is ....

Answer the questions.

3   Where is the dog?

....

4   What is the man doing?

....

Now write two sentences about the picture.

5   ....

6   ....

Speaking

Find the Differences

Picture Story

Clare and the monkey

monkey

Clare

Odd-one-out

Blank Page

Find the Differences

Picture Story

Don't worry! I've got a map!

Odd-one-out

Blank Page

Find the Differences

Picture Story

Charlie gets the teddy bear

Charlie

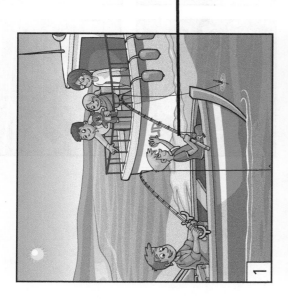

Odd-one-out